JERUSALEM OF GOLD

Jewish Stories of the Enchanted City

Retold by HOWARD SCHWARTZ

Illustrated by NEIL WALDMAN

For People of All Faiths, All Backgrounds

JEWISH LIGHTS Publishing

Woodstock, Vermont

Some of these stories have previously appeared in
Cricket, *Reform Judaism*, and *Shofar* magazines.

Special thanks to my editor, Deborah Brodie,
whose inspired vision sustained this project at every stage.

Thanks, too, to Arielle North Olson,
for assistance in the editing of these stories,
as well as to Carolyn Greene, Associate Executive Director,
Conference of Presidents of Major American Jewish
Organizations; Yocheved Herschlag Muffs, Judaica consultant;
and Dr. Jack Wertheimer, Professor of Jewish History at the
Jewish Theological Seminary of America, who read this text for
background authenticity.

Jerusalem of Gold:
Jewish Stories of the Enchanted City

2003 First Jewish Lights Publishing Edition

Library of Congress Cataloging-in-Publication Data
Schwartz, Howard, 1945–
[Next year in Jerusalem]
Jerusalem of gold : Jewish stories of the enchanted city / retold by Howard Schwartz ; illustrated by Neil Waldman.
      p.   cm.
Originally published under title: Next year in Jerusalem. New York : Viking, 1996.
Summary: Jewish stories set in Jerusalem, adapted from the Talmud and Midrash, Hasidic sources, and oral tradition, with origins in the Middle East, Eastern Europe, Spain, Italy, and Greece.
ISBN 1-58023-149-7
1. Legends, Jewish. 2. Legends—Jerusalem. 3. Jerusalem—Juvenile literature. 4. Aggada—Juvenile literature. 5. Hasidim—Legends. 6. Jews—Folklore. 7. Jerusalem—Folklore. [1. Jews—Folklore. 2. Jerusalem—Folklore. 3. Folklore.] I. Waldman, Neil, ill. II. Title.
BM530.S473 2003
296.4'82—dc21
                                                                          2003040026

Text © 1996 by Howard Schwartz
Illustrations © 1996 by Neil Waldman
Originally published as *Next Year in Jerusalem* by Viking, a division of Penguin Books USA, Inc.

10   9   8   7   6   5   4   3   2   1

Manufactured in Singapore

For People of All Faiths, All Backgrounds
Published by Jewish Lights Publishing
A Division of LongHill Partners, Inc.
Sunset Farm Offices, Route 4, P.O. Box 237
Woodstock, VT 05091
Tel: (802) 457-4000   Fax: (802) 457-4004
www.jewishlights.com

For Shira

Nathan

and Miriam

and for Tsila,
a native of Jerusalem

—H. S.

For Les Tourk, dear friend,
thank you for your insights and your honesty.
I have treasured our time together.

—N. W.

CONTENTS

INTRODUCTION   1

THE BIRD OF HAPPINESS   4

THE MOUNTAIN THAT MOVED   10

THE LANGUAGE OF THE BIRDS   14

HOW THE WALLS OF THE TEMPLE WERE BUILT   19

THE VAMPIRE DEMON   22

**THE STORY OF SERAH, WHO LIVED   26
LONGER THAN METHUSELAH**

THE PRINCESS OF LIGHT   32

CHALLAHS IN THE ARK   35

THE MIRACLE AT KING DAVID'S TOMB   39

RABBI NACHMAN'S CHAIR   44

MILK AND HONEY   48

GLOSSARY   57

SOURCES OF THE STORIES   58

INTRODUCTION

In ancient times, Jerusalem was often portrayed as the center of the world. After all, it is a city with holy places for the three major Western religions of Judaism, Christianity, and Islam. Many of the events that took place there are recorded in the Bible, especially in stories about King David and King Solomon.

Solomon built the Temple in Jerusalem, and it was the center of Jewish life for many centuries. But over the ages, control of Jerusalem has changed hands many times. It has been ruled at various times by the Jews, Romans, Muslims, and Christian Crusaders.

The city and its Temple were destroyed in 586 B.C.E. by the Babylonian conquerors, and many Jews were exiled to Babylon. Over the course of the next century, Jews began to return to the city and eventually rebuilt the Temple, which was destroyed for a second time by the Romans in 70 C.E.

Although the temple was torn down, one of its retaining walls, the Western Wall, still remains standing—angels are said to protect it with their wings. Today Jews come from all over the world to pray there, and many Jews consider it the most significant Jewish site in the world. It is a custom for visitors to the Western Wall to write messages to God, roll them up, and place them in the cracks of the Wall. Many miracles have been reported by those who have left messages there.

The city of Jerusalem has also been the subject of many Jewish stories. Some of these come from the great Jewish books that were written after the Bible, such as the Talmud and Midrash, where the legends of the

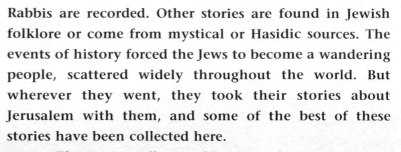

Rabbis are recorded. Other stories are found in Jewish folklore or come from mystical or Hasidic sources. The events of history forced the Jews to become a wandering people, scattered widely throughout the world. But wherever they went, they took their stories about Jerusalem with them, and some of the best of these stories have been collected here.

There are really two histories of Jerusalem. One is the actual history, and the other is a legendary one. In the stories in this book, we find a mixture of the historical and the legendary. "The Miracle at King David's Tomb," for example, reflects the historical reality of the Muslim conquest of Jerusalem, while in the same story the ghostly appearance of King David to the girl who is trapped in his tomb is legendary.

That is the wonderful thing about Jerusalem: it is a place where the historical and the legendary meet. A visitor to Jerusalem, wandering through its narrow streets and seeing the light reflected from its golden stones, soon understands why it is called "Jerusalem of Gold." For there is a kind of magic in Jerusalem. Ask anyone who has been there. This is the Jerusalem that has served as a beacon for the Jewish imagination for three thousand years. At the same time, historically Jerusalem was subject to numerous wars, and frequently conquered, leading to great hardship for the Jews. Jerusalem was denied to the Jews for centuries, but they kept its memory alive in story, legend, and prayer. And even to this day, Jews from all over the world proclaim at the end of the Passover seder and on Yom Kippur, the holiest day of the year, "Next year in Jerusalem!"

For more than seven hundred years before this century, Jerusalem was controlled by various Muslim rulers. In 1920 the British began to administer the area. By this time, Jerusalem had expanded beyond the walls of the Old City. In the 1948 War of Independence between Israel and the Arab states, which established the state of Israel, Jordan captured the Old City of Jerusalem, and the Jewish inhabitants were forced to flee. This resulted in Jerusalem being divided for the next nineteen years into the old walled city and the new city that had grown up around it. During this time, Jews were barred from entering the Old City of Jerusalem, and thus they could not visit the Western Wall, nor could they go to the synagogues there. But during the Six Day War in 1967, the Israel Defense Forces liberated the Old City, and Jerusalem was reunited. At that time, Jews flocked to the Wall and cried tears of joy that all of Jerusalem was once again accessible to the Jewish people. So, too, did they pray with great passion and write messages to God which they tucked into the cracks between the stones of the Wall.

Ever since, Jerusalem has been a city where all may freely practice their faiths, and the presence of all three major Western religions is quite apparent. And in 1996 the three thousandth anniversary of the founding of Jerusalem was celebrated, not only in Jerusalem but all over the world.

Today Jerusalem is a flourishing city where the ancient and the modern exist side by side. King David's tomb is not far from King David Street, where the King David Hotel can be found. Modern-day Israelis go about their daily lives speaking the ancient Hebrew tongue of their ancestors, despite the fact that Hebrew was not used as a spoken language for more than two thousand years. The ancient stories about Jerusalem have survived, too, deeply rooted in history and legend. And on the Sabbath, when all work comes to an end and prayers can be heard everywhere, one realizes that everything about Jerusalem is holy, even the dust under one's feet.

THE BIRD OF HAPPINESS

JEWISH FAIRY TALES

There once was a young boy named Aaron, who had spent his entire life wandering in the desert with his parents. His mother and father had been slaves, but they had run away to find a place where they could be free.

Every day they had to search for food and water. The sun beat down on their backs and the sand blew into their faces. Still, Aaron never lost hope, for his mother would say, "One day the Bird of Happiness will guide us to Jerusalem."

Every night when they stopped to rest, Aaron's father would teach him what it meant to be a Jew. They had no books, but Aaron's father remembered the Bible stories he had learned as a boy, and he remembered the Ten Commandments, and these he taught to his son. Aaron took them to heart and let them be his guide.

So it was that they wandered for many years, and still the desert stretched endlessly before them. Then one night, Aaron had a vivid dream, in which he was traveling with his parents in a sandstorm. The world grew dark while the storm swirled around them. They covered themselves completely and crouched low, waiting for the storm to end. But when it did, they found they were lost. Their footprints had been covered by sand. They could not tell where they had come from or where they should go.

Just when everything looked hopeless, Aaron saw something on the horizon. At first it was only a speck moving their way, but soon he saw that it was

In this story, a glowing jewel magically guides Aaron's family through the desert as they search for the mythical Bird of Happiness. There are strong echoes here of the Exodus from Egypt, when Moses led the Israelites, who had been freed from slavery, through the wilderness to the Promised Land. But even if "The Bird of Happiness" is rooted in history, it is still a fairy tale, for Jerusalem was founded many centuries after the Exodus, and it was never ruled by a king chosen by a bird.

There is also another way of reading this story, however, in which the glowing jewel that guides Aaron and his family represents the Torah, the first five books of the Bible, whose sacred teachings are the primary guide of the Jewish people. And the Bird of Happiness represents freedom, which everyone searches for, especially anyone who has been a slave. Read in this way, the story teaches us that the Torah can guide a person to freedom. So we see how even if fairy tales are not literally true, they still can teach great truths.

a beautiful white bird. Before long, it had flown over his head and dropped something from its beak into his hand.

That is when Aaron awoke and found that he was holding a glowing stone. He jumped up, amazed. Somehow he had kept the gift the white bird had given him in his dream.

When Aaron showed the stone to his parents and told them his dream, his mother said, "This means the Bird of Happiness is coming that much closer."

Aaron hung the glowing stone from a leather thong around his neck, and it proved to be a wonderful guide. For it glowed only when they were traveling in the right direction, and it went dark when they were not. Now they found their way to every oasis in the desert, where pools of fresh water were surrounded by trees bearing sweet fruit. Each time they came to such an oasis, they said a prayer of thanks.

After years of following the way of the stone through shifting sands and blazing sun, they finally came to the walls of a great city. And when they passed through the gates, they were surprised to see a huge crowd. Aaron's father asked the name of the city, and a man told him it was Jerusalem. Aaron and his parents were astonished. And when Aaron's father asked why everyone was standing in the streets, he was told that their king had died and his successor was about to be chosen.

"And how is the new king selected?" asked Aaron's father.

"We let the will of Heaven decide," said the man. "We release the rare Bird of Happiness, and the person it lands on becomes the next king. That is why everyone is outside—because the bird is about to make its choice."

Aaron's family looked into the sky, hardly able to believe they had arrived in Jerusalem and would finally see the bird they had sought so long. High above them, a bird was flying in great circles. Then it began spiraling down, and as it did, the stone Aaron wore glowed more brilliantly than ever before. Suddenly Aaron realized that the bird in the sky was the white bird he had seen in his dream. He was even more amazed when he saw it dive directly toward him and felt it land upon his head.

A great shout arose from the crowd, and Aaron was picked up and carried away, much to the alarm of his parents. They rushed after him all the way to the king's palace, where the boy was placed on the king's throne, with the Bird of Happiness still perched on his head and everyone bowing low before him. At first Aaron thought it must be a dream, but he felt the tug of the bird's talons in his hair and he knew that he was wide awake.

In the days that followed, Aaron was crowned in a great ceremony. He and his parents wore the robes of royalty, and every important question was brought before him to decide. All that Aaron had to guide him were the Ten Commandments that his father had taught him, and the glowing stone, which still hung from around his neck. Whenever he sought its guidance, the stone would glow if the answer was yes, and it would remain dark if the answer was no.

Aaron and his parents lived in luxury in the palace. No longer did they wonder where they would sleep at night or what they would eat. They thanked God for all their blessings—and especially

THE GLOWING STONE

The glowing jewel that Aaron wears in this story has a long history in Jewish folklore. The light that glows inside it is the light that was created on the first day of creation, when God said, Let there be light. *This was a sacred light, unlike the earthly light of the fourth day of creation, which came from the sun, the moon, and the stars. The sacred light of the first day disappeared when Adam and Eve ate the forbidden fruit of the Tree of Knowledge. But God saved a little bit of this light inside a glowing stone known as the* Tzohar, *and gave it to Adam and Eve as they left the Garden of Eden, to keep as a reminder of all they had left*

for the Bird of Happiness, which sang sweet songs to them from its golden cage next to the throne.

At first the nobles of Jerusalem were worried that the fate of the city was being entrusted to such a young boy. But as they listened to his decisions, they realized he was very wise. There was only one thing they could not understand. The young king had asked that a simple shack be built out of branches next to the palace. There he spent an hour each day—but no one knew what he did.

Finally, the king's vizier could not contain his curiosity. One afternoon, he spied on the young king inside the shack, and he saw that Aaron had taken off his royal robes and put on the rags he had been wearing when he was chosen to be king. He stood before a mirror, wearing those rags, for a long time. Then he dressed again in his royal robes and returned to the palace.

Now the vizier was more curious than ever. At last he decided to ask the young king about his strange actions. Aaron said, "I go into that shack and put on my old rags to remember where I came from. For only then can I know where I must go."

When the vizier heard this, he knew that heaven had truly blessed them with a wise young king. He served Aaron faithfully for many years after that.

Aaron ruled Jerusalem well, always remembered his origins, and gave thanks every day for the blessings that the Bird of Happiness had brought him.

Iraq, oral tradition

behind. They, in turn, gave the stone to their children, and it was passed down until it reached Noah, and eventually Abraham, who gave the Tzohar *to his son Isaac, who later gave it to his son Jacob. In this way the glowing stone reached King Solomon, who is said to have hung the* Tzohar *in the Temple he built in Jerusalem, but it disappeared after the Temple was destroyed. Still, it reappears in many stories in Jewish folklore, such as this one.*

THE MOUNTAIN THAT MOVED

DAVID AND GOLIATH

King David and his son King Solomon were the most celebrated kings in Jewish history. As a result, a great many stories grew up about their lives, including stories about their childhoods.

The most famous incident in David's youth was his battle with Goliath, a Philistine and a giant of a man. When King Saul was leading the Jews into battle against the Philistines, Goliath challenged the men of Israel to send one man to fight against him. If Goliath won, the Jews would become the servants of the Philistines. But if the Jews won, then the Philistines would become

Long before David became king in Jerusalem, he was a shepherd boy, leading his father's flock to green pastures and still waters. He cared for all the sheep tenderly, but he loved one lamb the very best. Her name was Rachel, and she was the friskiest of all the lambs born that spring. But she was innocent of the cruel ways of the world. She did not know that lions lay in wait for tender young lambs or that hungry eagles peered down from the sky above.

One day when David was playing his shepherd's harp, he closed his eyes, carried away by the beauty of the song. He did not see Rachel scamper away. The lamb stopped to nibble some grass. Then she saw greener grass just ahead. Step by step, she moved farther from the flock. She climbed to the top of a hill and trotted down the other side.

When David opened his eyes, he did not notice that the lamb was missing. But then he heard her frightened bleating. He ran up the hill and saw an eagle rise from the shadowed valley beyond, with poor Rachel clutched in its talons.

The eagle flew across the valley to a huge mountain that David had never seen before. The young shepherd raced after the eagle. When he reached the foot of the mountain, he began to climb. The grass growing there hardly seemed like grass at all. It was tough and tangled, tripping David as he struggled upward. But David leaned on his shepherd's staff, pulled his feet free, and continued to climb.

He finally reached a level place and saw the eagle perched on the highest peak, still clutching the lamb. David shouted at the eagle and struck his staff against the ground.

At that very moment, the earth began to shake, and—as impossible as it may seem—the mountain moved as if it had awakened.

The startled eagle dropped the lamb and flapped away. Rachel came tumbling down and David caught her. He held her close, bracing himself against the quaking of the earth.

When the ground stopped moving, he and the lamb explored the mountain, looking for the best way to climb down.

That is when David noticed that they were standing between two huge horns that grew upward between gigantic ears. They were not on a mountain at all!

In truth, they were standing on a mammoth wild sheep called a *re'em*. It is said that there are only two *re'em*s in the entire world, living on

their servants.

One look at Goliath put terror in the heart of every man, and no one was willing to face him. When David, who was a young shepherd, saw this, he offered to fight Goliath himself. No one thought he had a chance against the giant Philistine, but David took his shepherd's slingshot and bravely faced him, and slew Goliath. After that, King Saul invited David to stay at the king's court, and eventually David was anointed by the prophet Samuel and became Saul's successor as king.

opposite sides of the earth, and they meet together only once every seventy years. The *re'em* was traveling to that meeting, which was soon to take place.

The great *re'em* stretched, ready to continue its journey. David realized they must get off quickly, before it carried them away. Then, all at once, they heard the angry roar of a lion in the valley below. And even though the *re'em* was a thousand times larger than the lion, it bowed down, because the lion is the king of beasts.

Imagine what happened to David and Rachel when the *re'em* bowed. David barely managed to hold on to one giant horn, but the lamb slid down it, landing right in front of the lion. And just as the lion opened its jaws, David shouted and slid down the horn himself. He didn't want to confront a lion, but how could he desert Rachel?

The lion looked at him, blinked, and bowed.

Then, for the first time in his life, David realized his destiny. For just as the *re'em* bowed before the king of the beasts, the lion bowed before the shepherd who soon would become one of the greatest kings the world has ever known.

So the astonished boy picked up the lamb and hurried back to his flock.

And many years later, after David had become the king of Israel, who ruled from the holy city of Jerusalem, he wrote about this adventure in the Psalms, saying, *Save me from the lion's jaws, for You have answered me from the horns of the* re'em (Psalms 22:22).

Italy, ninth century

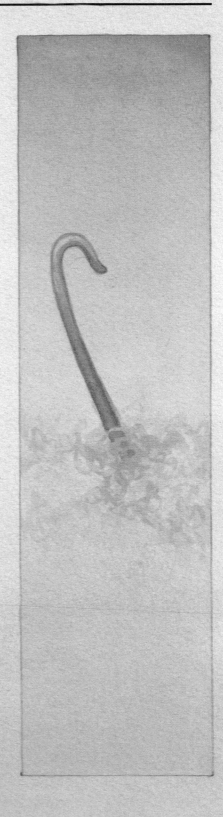

KING SOLOMON

THE LANGUAGE OF THE BIRDS

Solomon succeeded his father, King David, as king of Israel. He fulfilled the dream of his father by building a magnificent Temple in the city of Jerusalem. For about forty years, between 968 and 928 B.C.E., King Solomon ruled over a great kingdom, commanded a fleet of ships, and possessed vast amounts of gold and jewels. Many rulers of other kingdoms came to visit him, including the Queen of Sheba, and they brought him splendid gifts.

King Solomon was especially well known for his legendary wisdom. He was both a wise judge and a wise ruler, as well as a great poet and

Before he was king, when Solomon was still a young man and his father, King David, ruled over Jerusalem, Solomon sometimes left the palace and wandered through the streets of the city. He loved to walk in the crowded markets as much as he loved to walk alone in the fields and forests. Only one thing bothered him: wherever he went, people greeted him with great honor, for he was wearing his royal robes. But he wanted to be able to go among them without being recognized.

One day, while walking through the market, Solomon passed a young beggar. At that moment Solomon felt deeply ashamed that he should be so well dressed while the beggar boy had nothing but rags to wear. He went over to the boy and said, "I want to exchange clothes with you. I will give you everything I am wearing, if you will do the same." The young beggar could barely believe his good luck, so the two stepped behind a market stall and exchanged clothes at once. As soon as the beggar walked away, a crowd grew around him, for everyone thought he was a prince from a faraway land. They invited him to fine dinners in their homes, and as long as he wore those robes, he never went hungry.

Solomon, too, was delighted, for he had found a way to walk among the people and not be recognized. But imagine his surprise when the guard at the palace gate refused to let him in, saying, "Begone! I myself saw young Solomon leave the palace today, and he was not wearing tattered clothing. So you cannot be him."

Now Solomon might have had to sleep under a tree, but just then King David's general, Beneyahu, rode up to the palace on horseback. "Solomon, why are you dressed like that?" he asked.

"I am in disguise," Solomon said.

Beneyahu laughed. "Your disguise was almost too good."

When the guard heard this, he quickly opened the gate, and from then on he always recognized Solomon, no matter what he was wearing.

After that Solomon often left the palace dressed in rags. One day, as he was walking in a forest outside Jerusalem, he saw an old man sitting on a log. The old man sat there for a long time, turning his head from side to side, as if he were listening to a conversation. But no one else was there, except for the birds of the forest. Solomon was curious, so he went over and gave him the traditional greeting: *"Shalom aleichem."*

"Aleichem shalom, my prince," the old man said in reply.

"But how did you know who I am?" asked Solomon, greatly surprised.

"Why, the birds told me," the old man answered.

Solomon was astonished. "Can you understand the language of the birds?"

"Yes I can," said the old man. "Who do you think told me you were on your way?"

"The birds?" Solomon asked. The old man smiled. "And could you teach me their language?" The old man nodded his head.

They walked to the old man's cottage, deep

writer of parables. He was said to have been the author of three books of the Bible: Proverbs, the Song of Songs, and Ecclesiastes. He ruled during a time of peace, and greatly built up the city of Jerusalem, and even today he is regarded as the model of a great king.

STORIES ABOUT
KING SOLOMON

*Along with Elijah the
prophet, King Solomon is the
most popular figure in Jewish
folklore. But the King Solomon
of folklore is very different
from the King Solomon of the
Bible. As described in the
Bible, Solomon was an excep-
tionally wise and clever king
who ruled over a great and
widespread kingdom. In Jewish folklore, however, King
Solomon is portrayed as a
great sorcerer with unlimited
knowledge and powers, who
knows the languages of
the birds and of the winds.
He travels around on a flying carpet, and he is not
afraid to confront the forces
of the supernatural, such
as Asmodeus, the king of*

in the woods, and there Solomon began to learn the
secret language of the birds and many other mys-
teries. Solomon returned often, and before long, he
not only understood the birds, but he could speak
with them as well. So Solomon asked them, "Where
do you learn all your secrets?"

The birds replied, "We learn them from the
winds, who overhear the whispering of the angels."

Solomon was even more astonished than
before. "Could you teach me the language of the
winds?"

"Certainly," the birds all chirped at the same
time.

After that, Solomon went back to the forest
often, and the birds taught him the language of the
winds. So, too, did they teach him to call upon the
winds if he ever needed their help.

One day, when Solomon was returning to
Jerusalem, the birds warned him that danger
was nearby. He hid behind a large rock and
watched three men come down the road, laughing
and joking. They made their camp so close to
Solomon's hiding place that he could hear
everything they said.

"Let's climb into that tree across the road,"
said one.

"And drop down on any travelers who pass
by," said another.

"And take all their money," said the third,
roaring with laughter.

When the robbers climbed into the tree,
Solomon called upon the winds for help. Before
long there were winds rushing in from every
direction, north and south, east and west, shaking
the tree where the robbers were hiding. The

demons. This kind of transformation is typical of the way in which a historical figure, such as King Solomon, is changed into a hero of folklore.

branches shook so hard that the robbers fell down on the ground, and they ran off as fast as they could. After that they decided to repent of their sins, give back everything they had stolen, and become honest men. For they were certain that those mighty winds had been a warning sign from heaven to change their ways.

That is how Solomon learned not only the language of the birds but the language of the winds as well. And when he became king, he often called upon the birds and the winds for assistance. They told him everything he needed to know and helped him to overcome evil. Even to this day Solomon is known as the wisest of all kings, for he gained his wisdom from the chirping of the birds and the whispering of the winds.

Eastern Europe, nineteenth century

HOW THE WALLS
OF THE TEMPLE WERE BUILT

It was King David who first dreamed of building the Temple in Jerusalem. At night, in his dreams, he would climb Jacob's ladder until he reached the heavenly Jerusalem. For there is a Jerusalem in heaven that is the mirror image of the Jerusalem on earth.

King David was fascinated with the heavenly Temple, which was built at the beginning of time. In his dreams, he studied it from every side. So, too, did he explore every chamber of it. And when he awoke, he would write down the description of the heavenly Temple, for it was his plan to build one exactly like it in the city of Jerusalem.

During his lifetime, King David had the foundation of the Temple dug, but after his death it was up to his son King Solomon to see that it was built. So King Solomon called everyone together—the rich and the poor, the princes and the priests—and he said: "People of Israel, let us build a splendid Temple in Jerusalem in honor of God. And since the Temple will be the holy place of all the people, all of the people should share in building it. Therefore you will cast lots to decide which wall you will build."

So King Solomon prepared four lots. On one he wrote *North*, on another *South*, on the third *East*, and on the last *West*. Then he had each group choose one of them. In this way, it was decided that the princes would build the northern wall as well as the pillars and the stairs of the Temple. And the

Jerusalem is in the hills of Israel, and those who go there are said to "ascend to Jerusalem." The Hebrew term for this is aliyah, *which means "ascent." This term is also used in the synagogue, for those who are called upon to "ascend" to the pulpit, to participate in the reading of the Torah. At the same time,* aliyah *refers to the elevation of the soul. And it is also used by Jews living outside of Israel who decide to move there. They are said to "make* aliyah." *Thus the use of the term* aliyah *in connection with Jerusalem shows just how holy the city is considered to be. Many Jews regard the Western Wall as the most sacred place in the holy city of Jerusalem, and the place where God's presence can be most strongly felt.*

According to Jewish legends, there is not only an earthly Jerusalem but also a Jerusalem on high, a heavenly Jerusalem. And just as there was a Temple in Jerusalem before it was destroyed, so, too, is there one on high, which is eternal. Angels and the souls of the greatest sages fill the heavenly Temple, and the angel Michael is said to serve as high priest, offering up the prayers of Israel to God. Many Jewish stories recount journeys into Paradise, where the celestial Jerusalem can be found. Enoch was said to have made such a heavenly journey, and

priests would build the southern wall and tend the Ark and weave its curtain. As for the wealthy merchants, they were to build the eastern wall as well as supplying the oil that would burn for the Eternal Light. The job of building the western wall, as well as weaving the Temple's curtains, fell to the poor people, who also were to pray for the Temple's completion. Then the building began.

The merchants took the golden jewelry of their wives and sold it to pay workers to build the wall for them, and soon it was finished. Likewise the princes and the priests found ways to have their walls built for them. But the poor people, who had no money to pay for workers to help them, had to build the wall themselves, so it took them much longer.

Every day the poor came to the site of the Temple, and they worked with their own hands to build the western wall. And all the time they worked on it, their hearts were filled with joy, for their love of God was very great.

At last the Temple was finished, as beautiful as the Temple on high. Nothing in the world could compare with it, for it was the jewel in the crown of Jerusalem. And after that, whenever the poor people went to the Temple, fathers would say to their sons, "Do you see that stone in the wall? I put it there with my own hands." And mothers would say to their daughters, "Do you see that beautiful curtain in the Temple? I wove that curtain myself."

Many years later, when the Temple was destroyed, only the Western Wall was saved, for the angels spread their wings over it. For that wall, built by the poor, was the most precious of all in the eyes of God.

Even today the Western Wall is still standing. Now it is sometimes known as the Wailing Wall, for every morning drops of dew can be seen on its stones, and it is said among the people that the wall was crying at night for the Temple that was torn down.

And, as everyone who has been there can testify, God's presence can still be felt in that place.

Israel, oral tradition

Elijah was carried into heaven in a fiery chariot. These stories show the longing of the people to be closer to God, whose home is said to be in heaven.

THE VAMPIRE DEMON

Long, long ago, in the days when Solomon was king of Israel, he brought thousands of workers to Jerusalem to build the Holy Temple. Chief among them was the master builder of the Temple, who had a son named Benjamin whom he loved dearly. Indeed, the boy was so sweet and so clever that Solomon himself loved him as his own child.

Now King Solomon owned a ring on which God's Name was written, and with the help of this ring he could perform magic feats. Solomon had used this ring to capture Asmodeus, the king of demons, and because of this the demons were angry at King Solomon. They were also jealous of the Temple the king was building for the worship of God, and they decided to punish the king by stopping the building of the Temple. But how? They were afraid to make trouble for Solomon himself or for his chief builder, for those two were men of strength and wisdom. No! Instead, they decided to harm the young son of the builder. After all, how could a small boy fight the power of a demon?

So it was that one of the demons, called Ornais, was sent after the boy. One day, as Benjamin was on his way to visit his father, the demon suddenly appeared and bit him on the thumb and sucked the blood. The child became gravely ill. No one knew the cause of his illness and no one, not even the wisest of the king's doctors, knew how to cure him.

The builder was so greatly worried that he could not concentrate on his work, and without his guidance, the building of the holy Temple came to a halt. That was exactly what the demons wanted!

King Solomon, of course, was deeply worried, too. So he used his magic to find out what had caused the boy's strange illness. The king poured a little oil into his hand and saw in the oil an image of the evil demon biting the boy's thumb. Thus Solomon discovered what he must do. He went to visit the boy at once. He hugged him and assured him that the evil spirit who held him in its power was about to be destroyed. And then the king slipped off his magic ring with the secret Name of God inscribed on it.

"Wear this ring," the king told the boy, "and it will protect you from the demon. And if the demon ever comes near you again, slip the ring on the demon's finger. Then it will be in my power."

Not long afterward the demon sought out the boy again, for once a vampire has tasted blood, it wants to have more. The boy pretended to be asleep, but just as the demon was about to bite his thumb, he slipped the ring off his finger and onto the finger of the demon. This happened so fast that the demon did not realize what had happened. But when it tried to take off the ring, the ring would not budge. And when the demon saw the Name inscribed there, it knew that it had to obey the orders of the person who possessed the ring.

"Please, please," the demon begged, "don't force me to go to King Solomon." For it knew well to whom the ring belonged. But the boy commanded it to do so, and the demon had no choice but to obey.

When the boy brought the demon Ornais before the king, Solomon thanked the boy and told

DEMONS IN JEWISH LORE

From ancient times until about a century ago, most people, including the Jews, believed in the existence of demons, and also that there were ways to protect themselves. Now these beliefs are usually considered to be superstitions that were created to explain things people could not understand. Among the most famous demons in Jewish folklore are Asmodeus, the king of demons, and his queen, Lilith.

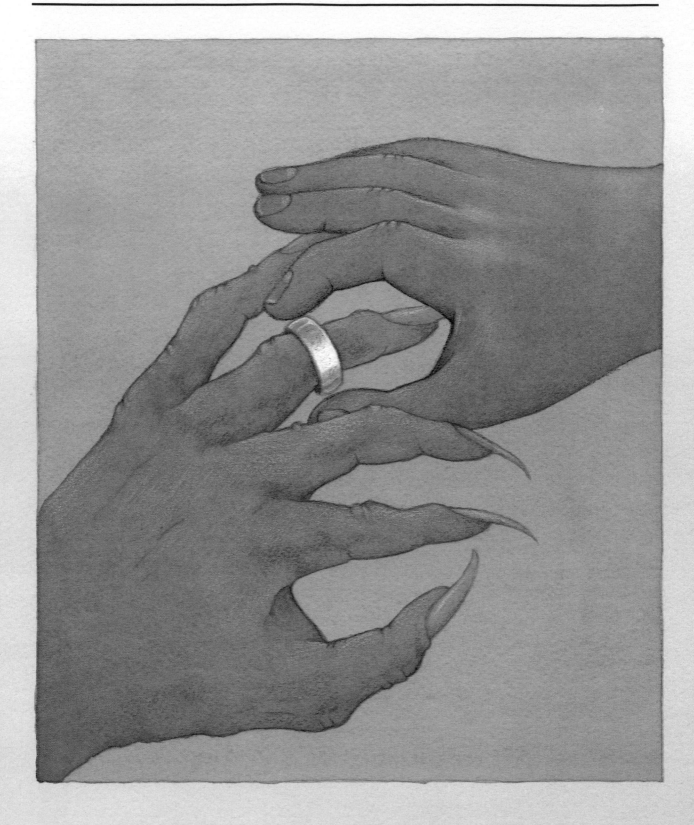

him that he had done well. Then Solomon questioned the demon harshly. "Why did you try to harm this boy?" And because the Name on the ring forced the demon to answer truthfully, it confessed all it had done. So, too, did King Solomon force the demon to reveal the names of all the other demons who had tried to spoil the building of the sacred Temple, and how to protect against them.

Then the king made a vow which was heard in this world and in the underworld as well. "I vow that the demon Ornais will remain my prisoner until the Temple is complete." And to ensure that this would happen, he commanded the demon to become a slave for the builder and carry the heavy stones for the Temple on its back. Not even the evil forces of all the demons put together could change Solomon's sacred oath. So the demons had to stop their efforts to harm the Temple, or Ornais would be a prisoner forever. And only when the entire Temple had been built did King Solomon set the demon free. Nor did that demon ever dare to harm a hair of anyone's head again.

By then the young boy had recovered from his illness, and he continued to serve King Solomon for many years in the very Temple that his father had helped to build.

Greece, circa first century C.E.

THE EXODUS

The Exodus of the Jewish people from Egypt, about 3500 years ago, is the great defining event of Jewish history. The Jewish people had come to Egypt during a famine, when Joseph was Pharaoh's chief advisor. But hundreds of years later, there was a new Pharaoh, and the Jews had been forced into slavery. Then Moses, at God's bidding, convinced Pharaoh to let the people go. Moses led them out of Egypt, as is recalled during the seder on the holiday of Passover. A great miracle took place at the Red Sea, when the waters parted and the people escaped the armies

THE STORY OF SERAH, WHO LIVED LONGER THAN METHUSELAH

Long ago, in the city of Jerusalem, lived a great rabbi whose name was Yohanan ben Zakkai. One day, as Rabbi Yohanan was teaching in the House of Study, an old woman stood outside the window and listened. She was listening to the rabbi discuss how the waters of the Red Sea had parted.

Rabbi Yohanan asked: "What did the walls of the Red Sea look like when the children of Israel passed through them?"

One student replied: "They looked like a waterfall." And Rabbi Yohanan said: "No, they did not look like that."

A second student said: "They looked like the pillars of the Temple." And Rabbi Yohanan said: "No, they did not look like that."

A third student said: "They looked like a window into the sea, where one could see schools of fish and all kinds of creatures of the sea." And Rabbi Yohanan said: "No, they did not look like that."

At last Rabbi Yohanan answered his own question. "What did the walls of the Red Sea look like? They looked like vines crisscrossing a window lattice."

All at once they heard a voice say, "No, it was not like that at all!" Everyone looked up, and they saw the old woman by the window.

"Who are you," Rabbi Yohanan said, "and how do you know what the walls of the Red Sea looked like?"

of Pharaoh that were pursuing them. So, too, did Moses lead them through the wilderness for forty years. In the defining moment of Jewish history, Moses climbed up Mount Sinai to receive the Torah, including the Ten Commandments, directly from God.

The old woman said, "I am Serah, the daughter of Asher and the granddaughter of Jacob, and I know what the walls looked like because I crossed the Red Sea!"

Now, Rabbi Yohanan knew that there was a Serah mentioned in the Bible, but that was very long ago. How could anyone live so long?

"If you are Serah, the daughter of Asher," he said, "you would be older than Methuselah, who lived more than nine hundred years."

"Indeed, I have lived longer than that," said Serah.

Rabbi Yohanan invited the old woman to come inside the House of Study. And when she was seated there, he said, "Surely you have a tale to tell."

"It is true," Serah began, "that I have lived very long and have seen a great many things. It all goes back to the time when I was seven years old.

"My father, Asher, and his brothers had just come back from Egypt with the news that their brother Joseph was alive. Indeed, he was known as the Prince of Egypt. And Joseph wanted everyone in the family to join him, for there was a famine in the land of Canaan, but there was food in Egypt.

"The time had come for my father and his brothers to tell their father, Jacob, that his son Joseph was alive. For many years, Jacob had believed that Joseph was dead. By then Jacob was an old man, and they were afraid the news would come as a great shock to him. So they asked me to play the harp and sing a song for my grandfather, and I was happy to do so.

"I went to the tent of my grandfather Jacob, and I played my harp and sang the words 'Joseph is alive, Joseph is alive,' as they had asked. At first my grandfather did not seem to notice me, for he was lost in his thoughts. But at last he listened to my song and jumped up. 'Is it true?' he asked. 'Is Joseph really alive?' I told him that it was true, and that Joseph was living in Egypt. Then my grandfather Jacob gave me a great blessing for bringing him such wonderful news. It is because of that blessing that I have lived so long."

Now, these words amazed Rabbi Yohanan and his students, for these things were not told in the Bible. They begged Serah to continue her tale.

"So it was that we went to Egypt," she said. "And as long as Joseph lived, our lives there were very good. But after Joseph died and a new Pharaoh came to rule, we were made into slaves. I, too, was a slave in Egypt.

"But at last Moses came and took us out of Egypt. I remember the last night we spent there. Moses had been gone all day, searching for the coffin of Joseph. For he knew that Joseph had wanted the Children of Israel to take his coffin with them when they left Egypt. But several hundred years had passed since then, and the people had forgotten where Joseph was buried.

"I saw Moses on his return, and he seemed very sad. I asked him what was wrong, and he told me that he couldn't find Joseph's coffin. I told him not to worry, for I knew where the coffin was hidden. He asked me who I was and how I knew, and I told him what I have told you. Then I led Moses to a place along the Nile, and I showed him where Joseph's golden coffin had been sunk into the river.

"Moses was happy to learn where Joseph's coffin was, but how could he raise it from the bottom of the Nile? So Moses went to the edge of

SERAH BAT ASHER

In the Bible, the name Serah bat Asher appears in two lists. The first, Genesis 46:17, lists Serah bat Asher as one of the sixty-nine Jews who accompanied Jacob into Egypt. In the second, Numbers 26:46, Serah's name appears in the census that Moses took in the wilderness, hundreds of years later. The Rabbis of the Talmud concluded that it was the same person, who lived so long because of the great blessing she had received from Jacob, her grandfather, when she told him the wonderful news that Joseph, his son, was still alive.

the river, leaned over, and said: 'Joseph, Joseph, we are leaving. If you want to come with us, come now. If not, we did our best.'

"Then a miracle took place. The golden coffin of Joseph floated to the surface, and when Moses bent over to pick it up, he found that it was as light as a feather, so happy were the bones of Joseph to return to the Holy Land.

"So it was that I crossed the Red Sea, as I have said. There were angels everywhere, watching over us, as we crossed. And the walls of the Red Sea looked like reflecting mirrors. And in those mirrors we not only saw ourselves but all the past and future generations as well. It was a wonderful sight!

"I also was among those who stood at Mount Sinai when the Torah was given. I can still hear the words of the Torah as Moses read them to us for the first time. After that, Moses carried the Tabernacle of the Law at the head of the caravan, next to the coffin of Joseph. For forty years, we wandered through the desert, until Joshua led us into the Holy Land. I was there, and I saw it all with my own eyes."

Rabbi Yohanan and his students were amazed to hear the story of Serah, the daughter of Asher. They realized how fortunate they were to have met her, for she was living proof that the words of the Bible were true. And in the days that followed, Serah came to that House of Study many times and told them wonderful tales about her long life.

Then one day Serah said good-bye, and set off once more on her wanderings. And some say she is still living among us.

Babylon, circa fifth century

RABBI YOHANAN BEN ZAKKAI

Rabbi Yohanan ben Zakkai was a great rabbi who lived in Jerusalem in the first century C.E. It was he who shaped many Jewish laws, and his authority was widely respected. According to legend, before the Temple in Jerusalem was destroyed in the year 70 C.E., Rabbi Yohanan had himself smuggled out of the city in a coffin, in order to set up a new academy for the study of the Torah in the town of Yavneh. In this way he was able to preserve Jewish education in a time of chaos and destruction. To this day there is a synagogue in the Jewish Quarter of Jerusalem, built in 1615, named for Rabbi Yohanan ben Zakkai.

THE SHEKHINAH

The central belief of the Jews is that there is only one God, who created the universe and established an eternal covenant with the Jewish people. In the Jewish view, God is not a man or a woman, but contains the qualities of both. In many parables, God is described as a king, as this was the closest earthly parallel to God's role.

The ancient Rabbis also called God's presence in this world the Shekhinah, which means the divine presence. This term originally referred to the sense of being in a sacred place. But in time, this idea changed, and by the thirteenth century the Shekhinah

THE PRINCESS OF LIGHT

Once upon a time, there was a princess who made her home in the Temple in Jerusalem. She was not a princess like any other, for she was made entirely of light.

Her father, the king, was ruler of the world and made his home in a heavenly palace. There he had two thrones, a throne of justice and a throne of mercy. When he sat on the throne of justice, he was a stern ruler, but when he sat on the throne of mercy, he was a forgiving one. The king had sent the princess into the world to give out blessings.

Most of the time this princess was invisible, although people could sense her presence, and once in a while they saw her in dreams and visions. Sometimes she appeared as a princess, sometimes as a bride, and sometimes as a divine presence that could be seen hovering over the Temple. Then people would say to each other, "Look, there is the princess!" Whenever they saw her, they always said a prayer, for they knew that as long as the princess was with them, her father, the king, was protecting them as well.

While the Temple stood in Jerusalem, the princess was happy, and her days were full of blessings. But when the Temple was torn down, the princess was heartbroken. She saw how the Jewish people she so loved were being forced to leave their land and go into exile, and she decided to go with them.

When her father, the king, learned that she had gone into exile, he called upon all the princes in the world to find her. And he told them: "Whoever finds my daughter, the princess, will wed her, and on the day of their wedding, the whole world will celebrate. But do not think it will be easy to find her. She is well hidden, but at the same time, she is always with her people."

Now, every prince wanted to wed the princess whose father was the ruler of the world. One by one, the bravest princes set out on a quest to find her, searching for her everywhere. They looked in every town and village, in every field and forest, in every room of every house and every nook and cranny. But even though they looked everywhere, they could not find her.

At last there was only one prince left who had not yet searched for the princess. Now it was his turn, and he could not turn down the quest. Before he set out into the world, he sat down in his royal chamber and said to himself, "Where is it that the princess is so well hidden, yet at the same time always with her people?"

This prince sought out a wise rabbi, and the rabbi said, "There is only one thing in the world that is always with the Jewish people, and that is the Torah."

Then the prince said, "In that case, can you teach me the Torah?" And the rabbi agreed to teach it to him.

Now the prince had to study the Torah for many years before he was able to master it, but a day came when he had become such a master of the Torah that he was able to find out where the princess was hidden. And, lo and behold, he found her there. Where did she hide herself? In the words of the Torah. For as he read the words of the Torah

was identified in many mystical parables as the bride of God, a queen, or, as in this story, a princess, whose home in this world was the Temple in Jerusalem, until it was destroyed. After that the Shekhinah was said to go into exile with her children, the Children of Israel. "The Princess of Light" is such a parable. The key to understanding this story and the idea of the Shekhinah is to remember that the Princess of Light is really God's presence in this world.

and understood the secrets hidden there, the wise prince suddenly glimpsed the light of the princess, and his eyes were filled with splendor.

And now that the prince knows where the princess is hidden, he is determined to set her free. And when he does, her father, the king, has promised to rebuild the Temple in Jerusalem that was once her home, and on the day of their wedding, the whole world will celebrate.

Spain, thirteenth century

CHALLAHS IN THE ARK

There once was a poor Jew named Yosef, who lived in the hills of Jerusalem. Even though he was poor, he was grateful for what he had—a little home for his wife and himself. And he wanted to give thanks to God.

One Sabbath, after saying the blessings, he took the first bite of the braided challah his wife had baked. The taste of this bread was so wonderful that he could not imagine a sweeter taste in this world or the next. Suddenly a thought occurred to Yosef. He asked his wife to bake two additional challahs for the next Sabbath, as an offering to God. His wife thought this was a wonderful idea, and she put her heart into making those two extra challahs. And all the while she kneaded the dough, the world seemed calm and at peace.

Early Friday morning, Yosef brought the two challahs to a little synagogue in the hills of Jerusalem not far from where he lived. It was so early that no one else was there. Then he opened the Ark, the cabinet where the Torah was kept, and put the two challahs inside it.

THE SABBATH

Genesis, the first book of the Bible, tells the story of how God created the world in six days and rested on the seventh. The Sabbath, coming on the seventh day, commemorates this day of rest, for on that day Jews are not supposed to do any kind of work. This is such an important day that the requirement to keep it is one of the Ten Commandments: Remember the Sabbath day to keep it holy.

Indeed, the Sabbath is one of the most important Jewish holy days. It is a day of joy in which all people are required to rest from their labors in order to

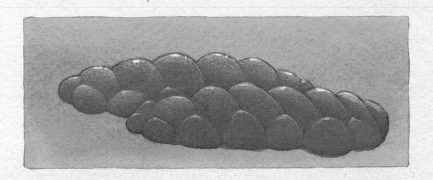

recover a sense of inner peace. The Rabbis of the Talmud believed that God's presence fills the world on the Sabbath. It is also believed that every Jew receives an extra soul on the Sabbath, which stays until the Sabbath is ended. The closing ceremony of the Sabbath is called Havdalah, which means "separation," for it separates the Sabbath from the rest of the week. There is a certain sadness associated with the end of the Sabbath, for then it is time to go back to the cares and burdens that were put aside during the Sabbath.

Later that morning the *shamash*, who took care of the synagogue, arrived, and he was struck at once by the wonderful aroma of freshly baked bread coming from the Ark. When he opened it and found the two challahs inside, he was quite astonished, for no one ever puts challahs in the Ark. Still, he saw how fresh they were, and he decided to deliver the challahs to the poor. It did not take him long to find two families without bread for the Sabbath. They blessed the *shamash* for the gift. Those were the sweetest challahs they had ever tasted, and made for the sweetest Sabbath.

Now, when Yosef came back to the synagogue on the morning of the Sabbath, he waited for the Ark to be opened, to see if his gift had been accepted. And when the doors of the Ark swung open, he was delighted to see that the challahs were no longer in the Ark. That was the happiest Sabbath of his life.

For the next Sabbath, Yosef's wife baked two more challahs, and Yosef delivered them, and the *shamash* gave them to the poor. This went on for several months, and Yosef and his wife were delighted that their gifts were seen as worthy by God. So, too, was the *shamash* happy to fulfill the commandment of giving charity. And the poor families who received those challahs celebrated the Sabbath with great joy.

But one Friday morning, the rabbi of that synagogue arrived early, and he saw Yosef opening the Ark and putting the loaves inside. Soon after that, the *shamash* arrived and took those loaves out of the Ark. Then the rabbi understood that Yosef was giving those loaves as an offering to God, and that the *shamash* was removing them.

GIVING CHARITY

Giving charity is one of the primary acts required by Judaism. The Hebrew term for charity is tzedakah. It is said that giving charity is equal in importance to all the other commandments combined. Indeed, it is considered a blessing to be able to give charity to another. For this reason, those needing charity have nothing to be ashamed of, because they are making it possible for others to perform a mitzvah, a good deed that is also a commandment.

The Bible directs us to be charitable; for example, farmers were to allow the poor to glean grains left in the fields. The concept behind the need to give charity is that fair treatment is deserved by all.

He confronted the *shamash*, who had the loaves in his hands, and demanded to know the truth. What was Yosef doing, and had he ever done it before? The *shamash* said, "Yes. He must be the one who has been bringing those challahs here for quite some time."

The rabbi said, "He is foolish to think that God wants such an offering, and you did wrong in making him think it was true."

Then the *shamash* said, "Come with me, and you can judge this matter for yourself." And though the rabbi did not know where he was being taken, he agreed to go.

So the *shamash* led the rabbi to the home of a poor family who could not afford to buy bread for the Sabbath, and he gave them one of the challahs. Then he took the second loaf to another family in need. When the rabbi saw how grateful they were, he understood that the gifts from Yosef and his wife were being directed by God to those poor people.

From that day on, the rabbi and the *shamash* watched Yosef bring that bread every week, and they smiled to themselves, wondering at the mysterious ways of God.

Israel, sixteenth century

THE MIRACLE
AT KING DAVID'S TOMB

KING DAVID'S TOMB

Long ago there was a young girl named Miriam. She lived with her mother in the Jewish quarter of Jerusalem. During the day, they sold fruits and vegetables at the market outside the city gates. At night Miriam would recite the Psalms and read books about the great heroes of old. She especially loved stories about King David, for she passed his tomb on Mount Zion every day on her way to the market.

At that time, Jerusalem was ruled by a cruel sheikh. He had passed a decree forbidding the Jews to pray at any of their holy places, including King David's tomb. Indeed, the punishment for any Jew caught inside David's tomb was death. This made Miriam sad, for she longed to honor the great king who was said to have written the beautiful Psalms that she so loved to read.

There was a kitten that used to play by the stall where Miriam and her mother worked. Miriam always brought some milk from home to give to the kitten. One day an evil man was passing through the market, when he noticed Miriam playing with the kitten. He saw how the girl loved it, and a dreadful plan occurred to him, for he was an enemy of the Jews.

That night, when Miriam and her mother had gone home, the man came back to the market, bringing a cup of milk with him. He went to Miriam's stall and called the kitten. When it came out to drink the milk, he grabbed it and threw it into a sack. Then he tied the top of the sack, carried

No one knows for certain where King David is really buried. The Bible says that he was buried in the "city of David," that is, in Jerusalem. The original tomb was probably destroyed during the Bar Kokhba revolt in 135 C.E. Over the centuries, various places were considered to be David's tomb, and for the past thousand years, it has been traditionally identified as the elaborate structure on Mount Zion in Israel, just outside the Zion gate, where this story takes place. For most of that time, the building was controlled by the Muslim rulers of Jerusalem, who refused to let Jews enter there. In the 1948 war between Israel and the Arabs, Mount Zion was captured by Israeli soldiers, and the shrine has been open to all ever since.

There are various tales about those who tried to enter King David's tomb and were confronted with the spirit of King David, who took revenge on them for disturbing his resting place. In this story, King David saves the Jewish girl who has been locked inside the tomb. The story reflects the Jewish frustration at being kept away from an important Jewish shrine, and also the tensions between Jews and Muslims during the long period in which the Muslims ruled Jerusalem.

it to King David's tomb, and tossed it inside.

The next day, as Miriam and her mother went to the market, they passed by King David's tomb and Miriam heard the meowing of a cat. Then, when they reached their stall, Miriam found that the kitten had disappeared, and no one knew what had happened to it.

Later that morning, the evil man returned to complete his plan. He purchased a large amount of fruits and vegetables from Miriam's mother, too much for him to carry himself. He offered to pay Miriam if she would help him, saying that his house was nearby, not far from King David's tomb. Since it was so close, Miriam's mother agreed to let her go, but made her promise to come right back.

As the man and Miriam made their way past King David's tomb, Miriam heard the meowing again, and this time she recognized the voice of her kitten. It must have somehow been shut inside the tomb. She wanted to run in and save it, but she knew it was forbidden. The evil man knew that his plan was working. He said, "I think I hear a cat crying from inside the tomb. Do you hear it?"

"Yes," said Miriam, "I do. And I'm certain it's my very own kitten."

"In that case," said the man, "why don't you run in and set it free?"

"But it's forbidden for me to be in there," said Miriam.

"Oh, don't worry," said the evil man, "no one will know. I'll wait here until you get back."

"Oh, thank you," cried Miriam. And without thinking about the danger involved, she rushed inside King David's tomb, where she saw the sack and heard the kitten crying inside. But just as she untied the sack, setting the kitten free, the gates of the tomb slammed shut. And then, to her horror, Miriam heard the evil man shouting that a Jew had slipped inside. A large crowd quickly gathered, and the man yelled, "Summon the sheikh's vizier, so he can see for himself how the Jews are disobeying the law of the land!"

Inside the tomb, Miriam burst into tears. The kitten rubbed against her ankles, but nothing could comfort her. She knew that she would lose her life if she were found there. How could such a terrible thing have happened? And she prayed with all her heart for God to help her. Then she started to recite the Psalms, for she had read them so many times that she knew them by heart.

All at once the tomb was lit up, and when Miriam raised her eyes, she saw a distinguished old man with a long white beard standing there. When Miriam saw his kindly face, she knew that he had come to save her. She picked up the kitten and joined the old man, who gently took her hand and led her down flights of stairs and along many passages. Finally she found herself standing on the other side of Mount Zion. "You are safe now," said the old man. "Hurry back to your mother, because she is very worried about you." Miriam asked the old man to tell her who he was, for she wanted to remember always who had saved her. The old man smiled and said, "King David."

When Miriam heard this, she trembled, for she realized that a miracle had truly taken place. There she was, standing in the presence of the great king. She took the hand of the old man and kissed it, and thanked him for saving her. Then she said good-bye to King David and rushed off, still carry-

STORIES ABOUT KING DAVID BEING ALIVE

Even though the Bible reports King David's death and burial, he was such a vital and important figure in Jewish history that many folktales arose in which he was reported to be alive. In some of these tales, he was said to be living in the city of Luz, a mythical city in the Holy Land where the Angel of Death was not permitted to enter. Some of the tales describe quests to this city to find King David in order to seek his help. One of the most popular Hebrew songs, David Melekh Yisrael, states that "David, King of Israel, still lives among us." In addition to these stories about King David, there are stories about such important

ing the kitten.

Meanwhile, the sheikh's vizier had arrived at the tomb with many soldiers. The evil man proudly told him how he had witnessed a Jewish girl slipping into the tomb, and how it was he who had shut the gate so that she could not escape. The vizier and the soldiers entered the tomb and looked for her. But no matter how long they searched, they could not find her.

At last the vizier emerged from the tomb, and his face was twisted with anger. He ordered the evil man to be arrested for making a false report. Only when the man gave up all his wealth was his life spared. He ran away from the city so that no one who knew him would see that he had become a beggar. And he was never seen again in the city of Jerusalem.

When Miriam reached the market, her mother wept tears of joy to see her, for she had just heard the reports that a Jewish girl was trapped in King David's tomb, and she was very worried. Miriam whispered the whole story in her mother's ear. When her mother heard how the evil man had tricked Miriam, she trembled with anger. But when she heard how King David had saved her daughter, she raised her arms to the heavens and gave thanks.

So Miriam and her mother lived happily after that, and her mother gladly let her bring the kitten to live with them. Every day was precious to them, for they had experienced a miracle they would never forget. And whenever Miriam recited the Psalms, she smiled, for she remembered how King David had saved her.

Israel, oral tradition

figures as Abraham, Moses, and Elijah the prophet appearing on earth long after their deaths.

RABBI NACHMAN'S CHAIR

One of the most remark-able developments in Jewish history took place in Eastern Europe in the eighteenth century. A poor Jew named Israel ben Eliezer, together with those he attracted as followers, created a move-ment of spiritual renewal within Judaism known as Hasidism. In time Israel ben Eliezer became known as the Baal Shem Tov, meaning the "Master of the Good Name," and Hasidism became so popular that nearly half the Jews living in Eastern Europe were Hasidic.

The Baal Shem Tov taught that the most important thing was not someone's

One of the greatest rabbis was Rabbi Nachman, who lived in the city of Bratslav. One of Rabbi Nachman's followers was a carpenter, and he devoted a year to carving a very beautiful chair for the rabbi. At last he gave the chair to him, and when Rabbi Nachman saw it, he was filled with delight. For that chair was as beautiful as any throne, and it was covered with intricate designs which the carpenter had carved himself. Rabbi Nachman thanked the carpenter with all his heart.

That night, Rabbi Nachman dreamed he was sitting on a throne in a palace, and people came from all over the world to see him. And when he awoke, he smiled at this dream, and he knew that he would always sit in that chair for as long as he lived.

After that, whenever Rabbi Nachman gathered his Hasidim around him, he always sat in that chair. Nor did anyone else dare to sit in it, for everyone knew that it belonged to the Rebbe, their leader.

On his deathbed, Rabbi Nachman called his Hasidim close to him and he whispered a secret. He said, "After I die, you will not need to find another rabbi, for I will always be with you."

His followers loved and trusted Rabbi Nachman so much that they did as he said, and they never appointed another rabbi. Instead they believed that the wandering spirit of Rabbi Nachman watched over them to protect them from danger.

Of course, his followers kept Rabbi Nachman's chair in an honored place, for it was a precious reminder to them of the Rebbe. No one else ever sat in the chair.

Time passed, and each generation of Rabbi Nachman's Hasidim kept that chair in their possession. Then during the Second World War, all the Jews of Eastern Europe found themselves in grave danger, including the followers of Rabbi Nachman. They learned that the Nazis were about to march on their city, and that they had very little time to escape.

All of Rabbi Nachman's Hasidim gathered together and decided that they would try to escape and make their way to the Holy Land, to the city of Jerusalem. There they would meet and build a synagogue where they would continue to follow the ways of Rabbi Nachman.

But there was one terrible problem. For while they could carry out sacred books and objects like *tallit* and *tefillin*, there was no way that they could take the chair with them. It was simply too big. Yet they could never leave it behind. What could they do?

While they were debating this, the young son of one of the Hasidim tugged at his father's sleeve and whispered in his ear. "Do you remember the Rebbe's story about the great stone?" he asked. His father's eyes opened wide, and he told the others what his son had said. The boy had remembered one of Rabbi Nachman's parables.

In this parable, a king decided to test his son, by asking him to carry a great millstone into the king's palace—by himself. The stone was so heavy that ten men could not lift it. For three days, the

knowledge but his or her depth of feeling, for God looks into the heart. So, too, he emphasized dancing, singing, joy, and the telling of stories as ways of becoming close to God. His teachings made it possible for peasants and others who lacked an education to feel that their prayers mattered as much as anyone else's.

Each circle of hasidim was led by a rabbi known as the Rebbe, whose followers considered him to be their master, and put themselves completely in his power, consulting with him on every decision. Hasidism differs from traditional Judaism in the emphasis it puts on the role of the Rebbe.

RABBI NACHMAN OF

BRATSLAV

Rabbi Nachman of Brat-slav (1772–1811) was the great-grandson of the Baal Shem Tov, the founder of Hasidism, and he is widely considered to be the greatest Jewish storyteller of all time. Rabbi Nachman told his followers that they would not need to appoint a new Rebbe after he died. Even to this day, the Bratslav Hasidim are thriving in Israel, and they still follow the teachings of Rabbi Nachman. The story recounted in "Rabbi Nachman's Chair" is said to be true, and the chair itself can be seen in the Bratslaver synagogue in Meah Shearim in Jerusalem.

prince sat next to that stone, wondering how he could accomplish such an impossible task. Then he noticed a squirrel breaking open a big nut so that it could carry it into its nest. All at once he had an idea, and he took a hammer and began to break the stone into pieces. When the pieces were small enough to be lifted, he easily carried them into the palace. And that is how he accomplished the impossible task.

When the other Hasidim were reminded of this tale, they clapped their hands together in delight, for they felt certain that Rabbi Nachman must have inspired the boy to think of that parable. They carved that beautiful chair into small pieces, and they gave one piece of it to each and every one of the Rebbe's followers, including the boy who had reminded them of the Rebbe's tale. Then they made a vow to set out for Jerusalem, and once they had arrived, to reassemble the chair.

Now in those dangerous times, there were few who escaped unharmed. But by a miracle, the wise boy and every other one of Rabbi Nachman's Hasidim who carried a piece of that chair arrived safely in the city of Jerusalem. There they reassembled it, with the help of a carpenter, and he did such a good job that no one could tell it had ever been broken apart.

That chair can be seen to this day in the Bratslaver synagogue in Jerusalem, where it has been placed beside the Ark. And among his followers, there is no doubt that it was the spirit of Rabbi Nachman who protected them in that time of danger, and led them safely to the holy city of Jerusalem.

Eastern Europe, oral tradition

MILK AND HONEY

Jewish history has been marked by many exiles from Eretz Yisrael, *the land of Israel, also known as "the Land of Milk and Honey" (Exodus 3:8). This is the land that God promised to Abraham, the land that it took Moses and the Children of Israel forty years of wandering to reach. For six hundred years, there was a Jewish nation in the land of Israel, ruled over by kings such as David and Solomon, until the Temple was destroyed. A second Temple was built, which was also torn down. Later, Jews would be forced out of Israel and into exile in many*

Not so long ago, a shepherd boy named Joshua lived in a forest near a little Polish village. All his life, he had heard stories about the wonders of the Holy Land, the Land of Milk and Honey. He dreamed of going there someday, as Joshua of the Bible had done when Moses appointed him to lead the Children of Israel to the Promised Land.

Each day the boy herded his family's goats through the forest to a clearing where they grazed. He let them wander wherever they wished, for they always returned at sunset. And while they grazed, Joshua sat beneath a tree and studied the page of the Talmud that his father had taught him the night before. But he preferred to play Sabbath songs on his wooden flute, dreaming of the gardens and orchards of the Holy Land, so far away.

When Joshua led the seven goats back home, his little sister Leah was waiting for him. She helped him with the milking and fed the dog, the cat, the chickens, and the dove, so that Joshua would have more time to teach her how to read.

At night, they sat side by side in front of the stove, while their father told them stories he himself had heard from his father and grandfather. There were tales of sages and heroes, of angels and demons, of witches and wizards, all of which Joshua loved. But most of all, he loved to hear tales about the holy city of Jerusalem. He was especially interested in such wonders as the Western Wall, where people left messages for God in the cracks between the stones. It was said that the presence of angels could be felt there.

One morning, Joshua's mother handed him a cup of goat's milk. He thought it was unusually sweet, as if it had honey in it. The rest of the family agreed that it was the best milk they had ever tasted, and they wondered which goat it had come from. Because Joshua had milked the goats that morning, he knew which one it was, a young goat that had disappeared the day before and had barely returned by sunset.

The goat wandered off the next day, and the day after, and continued to give that delicious milk. Joshua's father saved some for the family and sold the rest in the village nearby. One day he returned home with a remarkable tale: "An old woman who buys our milk was ill for a long time. She could not get out of bed. But then a miracle took place. She drank that special milk and recovered at once. I couldn't believe my eyes when she came to the door to greet me. She is sure the milk possesses great powers.

"Joshua, see if you can find out where that goat is grazing. Then take the whole herd there so all the goats will give wonderful milk." Joshua promised that he wouldn't let the young goat slip out of his sight.

The next day, Joshua tied a bell to the goat's collar. He watched the herd carefully until he began to play his flute. Then he closed his eyes for only a moment, carried away by the melody. And when he opened his eyes, the young goat had disappeared.

He could hear the goat's bell jingling in the forest, so he raced after it. He finally saw the goat just before it disappeared behind a bush. Joshua hurried to the bush, but when he looked behind it,

countries all over the world. Yet throughout the centuries, a small remnant of Jews always remained in the land of Israel.

The Jewish people never lost hope of making the land of Israel their home again. Meanwhile, in most countries, Jews experienced some kind of oppression, and the great Jewish dream was to return to the land promised in the Bible. "Milk and Honey" reflects this longing. Now, of course, the state of Israel has been established, and today more than four million Jews make their home there. And for many Jews who live elsewhere, there is still a longing for the Holy Land. That is why the words "Next year in Jerusalem!" ring out at every Passover seder.

ENCHANTED CAVES
IN JEWISH LORE

Jewish legends and tales are full of stories about enchanted caves that lead directly to the land of Israel. In these stories, the caves are hidden, but someone either knows about one or finds one by accident and travels to the land of Israel in a very short time. The stories about these caves reflect the people's great longing to reach the land of Israel, so far away.

It is also said that these caves were created for the bones of the righteous to roll through at the End of Days. According to Jewish lore, this will be the end of the world as we know it, when the dead will be resurrected, and all Jews will assemble in the

the goat was not there. Instead, he saw something very strange, a cave that he had never seen before. Moreover, it was unlike any other cave, for there was a dim but beautiful light glowing inside it. And deep within that cave, Joshua could hear the faint jingling of the goat's bell.

At first Joshua didn't want to enter the cave, but he knew he had to find out where the goat had been grazing. He stepped inside and carefully moved along the narrow passage. Sometimes he had to bend low, or even crawl, but mostly the cave was high enough for him to walk upright.

It was getting brighter in the cave, and Joshua saw that it was filled with crystalline rocks reflecting the light. He continued to hear the goat's bell, and before long he heard the echoes of another sound like the chant of distant prayers, even though Joshua was certain there were no synagogues nearby.

The further Joshua went into the cave, the lighter it became and the louder the prayers grew, until Joshua could begin to distinguish one prayer from another.

At last the light grew so bright that he knew he was approaching the other end of the cave. He hurried so he wouldn't lose track of the goat. But when he stepped out of the cave, Joshua was astonished to see that the forest where he had entered the cave had vanished. He was standing in a beautiful orchard, instead, with date and fig and olive trees. This amazed Joshua, for he had seen no such trees growing in Poland. He had only heard of them growing in the Holy Land. And there, beneath one of the date trees, grazed the young goat. He saw a synagogue not far from that orchard and realized

Holy Land. And they will get there by going through one of these enchanted caves. Then, according to Jewish tradition, the footsteps of the Messiah will be heard throughout the land, and the great Temple in Jerusalem will rise again in all its glory.

that this was the source of the prayers he heard in the cave.

Joshua walked over to the goat and petted it, while it continued to graze, perfectly at peace. As he stood there, the scent of dates was so enticing that Joshua reached up and picked one. He took a bite and decided it was the sweetest fruit he had ever eaten. Joshua understood that the goat must have been grazing there each day. But he could not figure out where he was, for he seemed to have come to another land.

Joshua decided to ask someone, so he tied the goat's rope to a date tree and walked to the synagogue. The services had ended and ten men came out the door. One walked in his direction, so Joshua greeted him. The man returned the greeting and said, "What strange clothes you are wearing, young man. I have not seen any like them since I left the Old Country."

This made Joshua more curious than ever about where he was. He said, "I am new here. Please tell me where I am, for surely this is the most beautiful land in the world."

"Why, this is the Holy Land," said the man. "Don't you know you are in the city of Jerusalem?"

Joshua's heart skipped a beat. Was it possible that he had reached the city of his dreams? But how could this be? He had traveled only a short distance through the cave, and the Holy Land was so far away. It must have been a miracle. But Joshua wanted to be sure, so he asked the man the way to the Western Wall.

"That is what most strangers ask," said the man. "Just follow this path past the synagogue, and soon you will reach the gates of the city. From

there, anyone can guide you to the Western Wall."
So Joshua thanked the man and hurried off in that
direction.

Before long, Joshua saw the majestic gate,
with crowds of people entering and departing.
He followed those who went inside, and found
himself walking next to an old man who was
wearing a white robe and carrying a staff. The
old man greeted him, "*Shalom aleichem.*" Then he
asked, "Where are you going?"

"*Aleichem shalom,*" Joshua said. "I want to
see the Western Wall."

The old man replied, "I am going there. Let
us go together."

So the old man led Joshua through the streets
of Jerusalem. They passed through the teeming
marketplace, where every kind of food was offered,
from raisins and dates to sweet-smelling oranges.
Everyone was buying and selling and bargaining.
Joshua felt at home here, for he had often accompanied his father to the market in his own village.
Joshua thought to himself that he could sell the
milk of his goat there and earn enough to buy
something to eat.

As the old man and the boy walked along,
they could hear the sound of prayers everywhere,
for there were many synagogues in that part of the
city. Joshua recognized all the prayers, but the
melodies were different from those in his village.
Still, the words of the prayers were the same. And
knowing those words made him feel at home in
that distant place.

All the way to the Western Wall, Joshua
wondered if he was dreaming, for it was hard to
believe he had taken such a miraculous journey. Yet

he found that he was beginning to miss his family, and he wished that they could be with him.

At last they came to the Western Wall. Joshua's heart leaped at the sight of it. Joshua and the old man hastened to the wall, where dozens of men and women had gathered, all pouring out their hearts and leaving messages for God in the cracks between the stones in the wall. With their tears, they implored God's help, and they mourned the destruction of the Temple and the scattering of the Jewish people all over the world.

Joshua stood close to the wall and kissed it, with tears rolling down his cheeks. He had been waiting all his life for that moment: to stand before that wall in the city of Jerusalem in the land that God had promised to Abraham so long ago. Looking up, Joshua thought he saw some kind of holy presence hovering above the wall, and he knew that he was in a very sacred place. At that moment, Joshua decided that he must leave a message there.

Joshua began to recite the prayers he knew so well, praying with a passion he had never known, certain that God was listening to every word. When he finished, he looked up and saw that the old man was writing a message, which he rolled up and left in a crack in the wall. He turned to Joshua and held out a pen and a slip of paper, as if he had read Joshua's mind. Joshua thanked him and wrote a letter in which he gave thanks to God for bringing him to that holy place, and begged God to bring his family to join him there. Then he, too, rolled up the message and put it in a crack in the wall.

At the very instant the message touched the wall, the goat in the orchard reared up and broke its rope. It rushed to the entrance of the cave and quickly passed through to the other side, going directly to Joshua's house.

When Joshua's parents saw that the young goat had come back without him, they were very worried. And when the goat ran back into the forest, his parents and his sister ran after it, calling out for Joshua. The family's animals, chickens, and dove hurried along beside them until they reached the enchanted cave.

Meanwhile, Joshua took his leave of the old man and went back to the date tree where he had

tied up the goat. He gasped when he found the rope was broken and the goat was missing. Where could it have gone? All at once he thought of the cave. He ran to the entrance just in time to see the goat running out, followed by a dove. Joshua embraced the goat, and as he did, he heard familiar voices. He ran inside the cave and was overjoyed to see his whole family there—his father, his mother, and his little sister. He rushed into their arms and they all shed tears of joy for they had been reunited. And their faithful animals were with them as well.

Then Joshua told them the astonishing news—that they had arrived in the heart of Jerusalem, where they had always dreamed of going. And when they saw the orchards of Jerusalem instead of the forests of Poland, they realized that a miracle had taken place, making their dream come true. They soon decided to stay in the Holy Land, in the holy city of Jerusalem. And their lives in that land were blessed, and it is said that they are still living there to this day.

Poland, oral tradition

GLOSSARY

All terms in this glossary are Hebrew unless otherwise noted.

aliyah (ah-lee-YAH or ah-LEE-yah; literally *going up*) Migration to the land of Israel. It is also used for "going up" to the platform to read from the Torah.

B.C.E. (English abbreviation for *Before the Common Era*) The term used by many Jewish people in place of B.C., referring to the years before the date considered the year one in the standard modern numbering. Thus 586 B.C.E. refers to exactly the same date as 586 B.C.

C.E. (English abbreviation for *Common Era*) The term used by many Jewish people in place of A.D., referring to the years after the date considered the year one in the standard modern numbering.

challah (hah-LA or HAH-luh) Bread, often braided, baked for festive meals on the Sabbath or holidays.

Eretz Yisrael (ER-etz Yis-ra-ALE or EHR-etz yis-RO-ale) The land of Israel.

Hasid (ha-SEED or HA-seed; plural *Hasidim*; literally *pious one*) A follower of Hasidism. Hasidim are usually disciples of a religious leader known as a Rebbe.

Hasidism (ha-SEED-ism or ha-seed-IS-um) A movement of spiritual revival in Judaism founded by the Baal Shem Tov in the eighteenth century. It emphasizes ways of becoming closer to God through prayer, dancing, singing, and storytelling.

Havdalah (hav-dal-LA or hav-DULL-uh; literally *to extinguish* or *to separate*) The ceremony performed at the end of the Sabbath, denoting the separation of the Sabbath from the rest of the week that follows.

Kotel (ko-TELL or KO-tell; literally *wall*) The Western Wall, which is the last existing retaining wall of the Temple in Jerusalem. *Hakotel hamaaravi* (ha-ma-ah-rah-VEE) is the full name, meaning *Western Wall*, but everyone simply refers to it as the *Kotel*.

mitzvah (mitz-VAH or MITZ-vuh; plural *mitzvot,* mitz-VOT) A divine commandment. There are 613 *mitzvot* listed in the Torah. The term has also come to mean a good deed.

Rebbe (REH-bee) Yiddish term used for Hasidic leaders and masters. It is a Yiddish form of *rabbi*.

seder (SAY-der) The special dinner held on the first one or two nights of Passover, which is the spring festival that commemorates the Exodus from Egypt and freedom from slavery.

tallit (tal-LEET) Prayer shawl worn during morning services.

tefillin (Tuh-feel-EEN or tuh-FILL-in) Leather boxes containing verses from the Torah, which traditional Jews wear on their heads and left arms during morning prayers.

Torah (Toe-RAH or TOE-rah) The Five Books of Moses: Genesis, Exodus, Leviticus, Numbers, and Deuteronomy. In a broader sense, the term refers to the whole Hebrew Bible and the Oral Law (the oral traditions that comment upon the written Torah). And in the broadest sense, it refers to all of Jewish culture and teaching.

tzedakah (Tsuh-dah-KAH or Tsuh-DOK-uh; literally *righteousness*) Charity.

SOURCES OF THE STORIES

All sources are in Hebrew unless otherwise noted.

THE BIRD OF HAPPINESS (Iraq). Israel Folktale Archives (IFA) 280, collected by Zvi Moshe Haimovitch from Josef Shmuli of Basra, Iraq.

THE MOUNTAIN THAT MOVED (Italy). From *Midrash Tehillim*, 22:28.

THE LANGUAGE OF THE BIRDS (Eastern Europe). From *Sippure Tzaddikim*. Cracow: 1886. Also in *Lamed Vav Tzaddikim Nistarim*, edited by Yisrael Yaakov Klapholtz. Tel Aviv: 1968.

HOW THE WALLS OF THE TEMPLE WERE BUILT (Israel). From Zev Vilnay, *Aggadot Eretz Yisrael*, 4th edition (no. 193). Jerusalem: 1953. Collected by Zev Vilnay from a Jewish youth in Jerusalem in 1922.

THE VAMPIRE DEMON (Greece). From *The Testament of Solomon* (Greek), edition of F. F. Fleck, in *Wissenschaftliche Reise durch das sudliche Deutschland, Italien, Sicilien und Frankreich*, Volume 2, pp. 113–140. Leipzig: 1837.

THE STORY OF SERAH, WHO LIVED LONGER THAN METHUSELAH (Babylon). The account of Serah and the walls of the Red Sea is found in *Pesikta de-Rab Kahana* 11:13. The legend of Serah informing Jacob that Joseph is alive is from *Sefer Yashar*. Venice: 1613, 109b–110a. The legend about Serah revealing the location of the coffin of Joseph is found in *Mekilta de-Rabbi Ishmael*, Bashallah 24a–b, and in the Babylonian Talmud, Sota 13a–b, based on Exodus 13:19, "And Moses took the bones of Joseph with him."

THE PRINCESS OF LIGHT (Spain). Based on the myth of the exile of the *Shekhinah* in Zohar I:202b–203a and "The Lost Princess" from *Sippure Ma'aysiot* by Rabbi Nachman of Bratslav, edited by Rabbi Nathan Sternhartz of Nemirov. Warsaw: 1881.

CHALLAHS IN THE ARK (Israel). From *Shivhei ha-Ari*, edited by Shlomo Meinsterl. Jerusalem: 1905.

THE MIRACLE AT KING DAVID'S TOMB (Israel). Based on a legend collected by S. Z. Kahana, curator of Mount Zion, in *Legends of Zion*. Jerusalem: 1974.

RABBI NACHMAN'S CHAIR (Eastern Europe). Collected by Howard Schwartz from Yehuda Yaari. The dream is recorded in *Sippurim Hadashim* in *Hayey Moharan* by Rabbi Nathan of Nemerov, edited by Rabbi Nachman Goldstein of Tcherin. Lemberg: 1874. The parable of the millstone is from *Sippure Ma'aysiot Hadashim*, attributed to Rabbi Nachman of Bratslav. Warsaw: 1909.

MILK AND HONEY (Poland). As remembered by Dov Noy. IFA 532. This tale exists in several oral variants, including IFA 5842, collected by Rachel Seri, edited by Aliza Shenhar in *Ha-Kamea ha-Kadosh*, no. 11. A variant is found in *Yiddisher Folklor* (Yiddish), edited by Y. L. Cahan (1938), no. 20, p. 147.

Other Jewish Lights Books You May Enjoy

By Sandy Eisenberg Sasso

But God Remembered
Stories of Women from Creation to the Promised Land
Four lively stories of strong and courageous women from ancient tradition.
For ages 8 & up. 32 pp, full-color illus., HC,
ISBN 1-879045-43-5, $16.95

Noah's Wife
The Story of Naamah
A new story celebrating the wisdom of Naamah, whom God calls on to save each plant on Earth in the Great Flood.
For ages 4 & up. 32 pp, full-color illus., HC,
ISBN 1-58023-134-9, $16.95
Also available—a board book version for ages 0–4:
Naamah, Noah's Wife ISBN 1-893361-56-X, $7.95
A SKYLIGHT PATHS book

For Heaven's Sake
Isaiah, a young boy, searches for heaven and learns that it is often found in the places where you least expect it.
For ages 4 & up. 32 pp, full-color illus., HC,
ISBN 1-58023-054-7, $16.95

Cain & Abel •AWARD WINNER•
Finding the Fruits of Peace
A beautiful recasting of the biblical tale. A spiritual conversation-starter about anger and how to deal with it, for parents and children to share.
Ages 5 & up. 32 pp, full-color illus., HC,
ISBN 1-58023-123-3, $16.95

God in Between •AWARD WINNER•
If you wanted to find God, where would you look?
Teaches that God can be found where we are.
For ages 4 & up. 32 pp, full-color illus., HC,
ISBN 1-879045-86-9, $16.95

God's Paintbrush
Invites children of all faiths and backgrounds to encounter God through moments in their own lives, and gives adult and child questions for exploring their faith together. Interactive.
For ages 4 & up. 32 pp, full-color illus., HC,
ISBN 1-879045-22-2, $16.95

God's Paintbrush Celebration Kit
A Spiritual Activity Kit for Teachers and Students of All Faiths, All Backgrounds
With delightful illustrations and activity sheets to encourage discussion, this indispensable, completely nonsectarian teaching tool is designed for religious education settings in church and synagogue alike.
Five sessions for eight children ages 5–8. 40 full-color activity sheets and teacher folder, ISBN 1-58023-050-4, $21.95

God Said Amen
A stubborn Prince and Princess show children and adults how self-centered actions affect the people around us, and how by working together we can work with God—to create a better world.
For ages 4 & up. 32 pp, full-color illus., HC,
ISBN 1-58023-080-6, $16.95

In God's Name •AWARD WINNER•
What is God's name? The story of people who set out to find the answer. Celebrates the ultimate harmony of belief in one God by people of all faiths.
For ages 4 & up. 32 pp, full-color illus., HC,
ISBN 1-879045-26-5, $16.95
Also available—a board book version for ages 0–4:
What Is God's Name? ISBN 1-893361-10-1, $7.95
A SKYLIGHT PATHS book

In God's Name is also available in Spanish:
El nombre de Dios 32 pp, full-color illus., HC,
ISBN 1-893361-63-2, $16.95